The Needle

Also by Jennifer Grotz

CUSP

The Needle

Poems

Jennifer Grotz

Houghton Mifflin Harcourt
BOSTON   NEW YORK
2011

For information about permission to reproduce selections from this book,
write to Permissions, Houghton Mifflin Harcourt Publishing Company,
215 Park Avenue South, New York, New York 10003.

www.hmhbooks.com

Library of Congress Cataloging-in-Publication Data
Grotz, Jennifer.
The needle : poems / Jennifer Grotz.
p. cm.
ISBN 978-0-547-44412-3
I. Title.
PS3607.R675N44 2010
811'.6 — c22   2010025570

Book design by Brian Moore

Printed in the United States of America

DOC 10 9 8 7 6 5 4 3 2 1

To take objects out of their royal silence, one
must use either a stratagem or a crime.

—ZBIGNIEW HERBERT

Contents

III

The Needle

"When your eyes have done their part,
Thought must length it in the heart."
—SAMUEL DANIEL

. . . Thought lengths it, pulls
an invisible world through
a needle's eye
                one detail at a time,

beginning with
the glint of blond down
on his knuckle as he
                crushed a spent cigarette—

I can see that last strand of smoke
escaping in a tiny gasp—above the table where
a bee fed thoughtfully
                from a bowl of sugar.

World of shadows! where
his thumb lodged into
the belly of an apple,
                then split it in two,

releasing the scent that exists
only in late summer's apples
as we bit into
                rough halves flooded with juice.

Memory meticulously stitches
the market square
where stalls of fruit
                    ripened in the heat.

Stitches the shadows stretched and
pulled across the ground by
the crowds pigeons
                    seemed to mimic

in their self-important
but not quite purposeful
strutting,
            singly and in droves.

Stitches the unraveling
world where
only vendors and policemen
                    stood in place.

I

The Icon

Beginning with gold around the edges
and ending with the eyes' sorrowful gaze,

the face of a Madonna with child
makes a dark mirror of what you are to feel:

the temporary but desperate way
a part of you is wounded

until the hurt becomes a lens. Inside you is a city
the mosaic spells out with tiny precious stones

across the ceiling and the walls.
And the city has its currency: every tessera is a coin

you must struggle to spend by looking,
the way rain slowly covers every cobblestone on a street.

A camera won't work: the tourists' feeble flashes
cannot ascend high enough, cannot take in

the Madonna's head tilted in thought,
the baby happy and silent like a secret.

Landscape with Town Square

One way to survive is to be a little piece of scenery
Among the mirabilia of the square, spending one's time

In an outdoor café while a weather system of people
Drips ice cream on the ground. At day's end you leave

Simply for the pleasure of the next morning's return,
Of rounding the corner to see the jostled chessboard of tourists
Underneath the church's towers.

Every day the breakdancers come with their pathetic boom box
To spin and convulse and do whatever gymnastics they can muster

Next to the requisite sad accordion-player, and even a gypsy
Who beseeches and curses bewildered passersby.

On one corner, a tiny ancient church keeps its doors open,
Letting a summer carnival enter the dark altar

While, just outside, the soap blowers wave wands long as fishing poles,
Gingerly releasing the huge trembling globes
Which rise fiery and iridescent like souls.

So stubbornly do we congregate that even in lightning and thunder
We sit strangely unalarmed, eating our chilling omelets
While canvas umbrellas flap and the rain sprays our tables in gusts.

And afterward, the wet and gleaming square seems slowly rubbed dry
By the bolt of blue-gray velvet the sky unspools above.

It is hard to know which view is really reality: the square itself, wiped clean
Of all the people, or the incomprehensible shuffling of the people

Who are incomprehensible and shuffling all over the world, all the time.
Either view scours the heart, keeps down its wild romantic notions.

Alchemy

All day the city went on being a city we traversed
as if it could be conquered by touch,

leaning against stone walls and wrapping our fingers
around rails overlooking the river.

And all through the city, the day went on being a day
blazing ruthlessly, even when it started to rain,

and the devil beat his daughter all afternoon
until sparrows stirred the cauldron of sky

and dusk doused the flames in greenish smoke.
That was more or less the recipe to make night,

when the city writes its unspendable wealth inside us.
When a pebble becomes a bright coin on the sidewalk,

where a black ermine scurries under a car
to replace motor oil rushing into the gutter.

And I become a bird squeezed in a boy's dirty palms
while you digest an iron egg of dread,

the empirical result whenever moonlight
takes shadow to be her lawfully wedded husband.

One's fate in this city is to come and become and be overcome.
In each of us a mad rabbit thrashes and a wolf pack howls.

The Pearl

You were seen once, in a dim light.
Two hands held your face and then two blue eyes

met yours, you could see them in the act of looking
and then you saw them see at the same time you felt it,

that you were being seen
and not until this happened did you know

this was something you required and also
that each of you had become a stranger.

Then you understood why animals take looking
as a sign of aggression. Two pairs of eyes

struggled against each other. And also the stranger's hand
behind your ear, but no memory of the back of the earring

sliding off, just of your own eyes
exhausting themselves in a looking back

you could almost translate, if you could say simultaneously
I am starving and *I am not afraid of you.*

There was nothing like agreement. It might even have been a war.
The eyes did not relent, not until dawn arrived

and you were alone again, when you began to imagine
sleep was the stranger returning

and only then allowed its delicious possession
to overtake you. It cost one pearl.

The Sidewalk

Amid foot traffic and cars, morning sun blares off storefront windows
while workers are digging up the sidewalk. Waist-deep in the ground,
one of them holds something up for the others to see.

Everything halts as they inspect it: round, crusted with earth, crumbling.
Even the pigeons seem curious, gathering at the lip of the hole,
adjusting their footing on the spill of rocks to crowd in for a look.

Look how carefully the workers hold their discovery,
passing it back and forth, no one wanting to set it on the ground,
the tone of their voices tense as they discuss what it is, what to do.

I can't make out their words, but I am thinking about an actor
who bequeathed his own skull to the Royal Shakespeare Company
to serve as Yorick's in the graveyard scene,

wanting perhaps to serve later Hamlets in this modest way,
having spent many nights holding up a plaster copy
and looking deep into the empty eye sockets, open jaw.

Buried underground, what if we are just as lonely. Surely
in death we are still misunderstood. Too brittle to use on stage,
the actor's skull was put away in a glass case.

Late Summer

Before the moths have even appeared
to orbit around them, the streetlamps come on,
a long row of them glowing uselessly

along the ring of garden that circles the city center,
where your steps count down the dulling of daylight.
At your feet, a bee crawls in small circles like a toy unwinding.

Summer specializes in time, slows it down almost to dream.
And the noisy day goes so quiet you can hear
the bedraggled man who visits each trash receptacle

mutter in disbelief: *Everything in the world is being thrown away!*
Summer lingers, but it's about ending. It's about how things
redden and ripen and burst and come down. It's when

city workers cut down trees, demolishing
one limb at a time, spilling the crumbs
of twigs and leaves all over the tablecloth of street.

Sunglasses! the man softly exclaims
while beside him blooms a large gray rose of pigeons
huddled around a dropped piece of bread.

The Nunnery

Today on the tram, I give up my seat to a nun
wearing a Members Only jacket. I watch her

the way you watch someone who
doesn't know she's being stared at, as if

trying to *learn* her, you see it all the time
on the tram, the way each person in the car

takes turns waking from the momentary hibernation
of public transportation to stare at the others,

our fascination at the blank and pensive faces on the tram—
I admit it, I'm looking for clues of what it's like to be a nun.

Nuns roam the streets of Krakow like the rest of us,
singly and in pairs, and sometimes like a school of fish

that shifts and undulates while it pours
like a holy liquid through the city.

She balances her purse squarely on her lap. Then touches her habit
absent-mindedly while looking out the window.

Nobody I know would take advice from Hamlet. The closest I ever
got myself was next door to a nunnery,

in a fifth-floor walkup overlooking the convent garden.
It was an orchard carpeted with clover lush as baby's hair.

In the mornings the nuns would file through the green of it
to the sound of bells. In late summer, wind

sent the apples down in soft thuds. When they were away,
a neat row of straw baskets stained from berry picking remained.

Boy Playing Violin

There's a boy playing the violin in the corner of the square.
The sounds coming from his violin are awful — is that supposed to be
Mozart? — and he looks ready to burst into tears.
The bowl on the ground in front of him is empty — unbelievable

when you see his competition, a middle-aged man with a boom box
and a marionette of Elvis whose hips he thrusts dramatically
to "You Ain't Nothing but a Hound Dog."
The puppeteer has the advantage of real estate,

having staked out a spot right in the center of the square,
but the boy knows what to do —
he sets up in front of the cathedral and steals some flowers
from the vendors nearby to strew on the ground.

So the puppeteer responds by pulling out a Tina Turner puppet
with little silver high heels and a bona fide snarl,
jacking up the volume to "What's Love Got to Do with It?"
to drown out the squeaks of the boy's violin.

The next day the boy has traded in his violin for an accordion
that he opens and shuts like a giant Slinky, his music a palpable
but unintelligible sighing about the misery of childhood, reinforced by
a thirsty puppy propped on a pillow in front of him.

If this were Virgil, now is when
an older, wiser song-maker would intervene,
coming to judge and anoint the victor with his own reed.
But this is a city square populated by potbellied men

with cameras strapped around their neck,
their well-appointed wives accessorized with globules of amber,
and by lovers holding hands, oblivious,
and by waddling pigeons chased endlessly

by children, and, gentle reader, by
poetry waiting like a beautiful woman
no one at the party will talk to,
like the carillon of ice shifting in her glass.

The Umbrella

The clouds grew thick the way gray fur
tints the last of the raspberries, the way
fingertips obscure a pane of glass.
Then pedestrians inflated their umbrellas
and the sidewalk bloomed.
It poured until it wasn't rain anymore
but something one endured with feeling,
deafening as laughter in a crowded bar
but equally awful because it made time stutter
in between day and night, city and sky.
We stood together, sharing an umbrella.
You held it above me, drenching your left shoulder,
unaware of the cold stream slicking off the canvas
down my back. When you asked why I gasped,
I didn't say a word, happy
to wait with you under an umbrella
until the sky proceeded elsewhere
escorted by the wind.

Not Body

When silence is a small quick word
that keeps being said. When lips
open to tongue. Silence punctuates
a spitting, a glowing wick,
wax warping to drape you
like a hood. You grow wild,

become a stubbornness.
Something like a whisper keeps coming forward.
Such a busy flame, leveling everything
to a hardened pool.
I'll keep the vigil.

Let a little light come tell me what.
Let a flicker make me brave.

I've always insisted on you. If I could
be sure. If the night were safe, not slippery
like a flame. If the body were more than a clock.
If the body could be seen through like a window.
If the body lives to be burned.

Then you: unpredictable and loyal. Then you:
snuffed out, or replaced
with the sweet valedictions of smoke.

The Cigarette

Like one who retraces
her steps to retrieve
something lost, I go back,
I go back when I hear
the tiny hiss of the cigarette
extinguished by the rain,
a slur of wet wheels on pavement,
remembering the cab
winding its way in reverse
down the deserted
one-way street. I go back
to the driver looking past us
in the back seat, the two
he had just rescued from
the downpour. The engine
straining in first gear goes back,
past the trembling lindens,
past the leaping flames
of the late-night kielbasa stand.
And before that, on foot, in fits
and starts my mind retraces
the shortcut through the park,
the ATM machine glowing on the corner,
unwinds the curving
cobblestone streets to the spot
where a kiss unfolded, even
the kiss unfolding in the mind
like a map one explores for
once-known territories. Still

it can't be found. What
the mind knows was there. That place
beneath a white volume of cloud
where one fiery breath turned
into water, turned going
forward into going back.

The Staircase

The city would begin as slowly as the old man in a brown fedora
making his way down the street, a walking stick in one hand
and the arm of the elderly woman beside him in the other. You
could catch them traversing the same sidewalk every morning

except for today, interrupted by plastic construction tape
knotted to a tree announcing the sidewalk closed. No
observable reason why—nothing's been done yet
by the worker leaning on his van, which is why

the two of them decide to go through anyhow,
and a graceless shimmy under the tape commences,
as if they are sneaking across the finish line
of the hardest, longest race in the world,

delightful to see until he begins to topple
and she is able to slow his fall for a moment
until she teeters and goes down with him
and even the walking stick falls over

by the time the worker hangs up his cell phone to help them
and the stray dog uses this moment to lift its leg
on the corner tire of the van instead of
the fence surrounding the tulips he normally visits,

the little stand that looks this morning like candles
whose wicks have all gone out.
This is how walking was a kind of thinking
you could practice all day long. Wind

wrinkled puddles on the sidewalk and nuns
swung their purses in the square
and drunks slept fitfully on benches while you
pondered the city in your impractical shoes,

not beholding from afar or above, but there,
yes, you too waited at the intersection
and faced the crowd across the street,
and when the light changed all of you

walked into each other
like a shuffling deck of cards
and the city became a feeling, an intricate thing
that could be expressed only with its entire self.

If, when you looked about, no one stepped forward,
still the feeling was not just yours.
Just yours was the mind on the staircase
at the end of the day,

when climbing was a kind of counting,
a slow unwinding upward to your fifth-floor flat.
Oh those one hundred steps were wooden, polished
to slipperiness, and objectively waiting

to annihilate any emotion into a gulp for air.
Zigzagging back and forth in ascending indecision,
you counted the day like a rich man hoarding every coin,
but nothing quite allowed itself

to be counted — a pigeon, was that one? The old man toppling
in the street? The smell of lindens at four in the afternoon?
Did that count? — everything converting back into the city
not to be counted but, like the bellies of stones, revealed.

II

The Window at Night

Eyes wide like an owl's, an aspirin-pale face
foretells in lamplight how it accumulates age.
Somewhat masked, somewhat naked, there's no way
to know what others see when looking at it.
All five of the body's senses crowd
on this small planet a weather of hair surrounds.

My face is not a democracy — the eyes are tyrants
and the ears are radical dissenters.
In the conversations of eyebrows, mine are whispers.
Like the window at night, the face reflects too,
uncertain how to change when greeting itself
(and is it not cruel when another's face
won't reflect acknowledgment of you?).

My mother, my father, and my brother are found
in the blurring of feature and expression.
Cynicism finds no purchase here;
the same cannot be said for sadness
(and look deeper — anger hides in the jaw).
And while the nose quietly broods
like an actor rehearsing his soliloquy,
the empty page of the forehead, when I raise my brows,
fills suddenly with questions.

Silence

I mothered you, I protected you,
you were my baby, my toy,
so there was no need for you to speak
when, at the dinner table, our mother asked
would you like some green beans
because I would answer, "No thank you,
but he'd like another helping of mashed potatoes."
Years later you assured me I always got it right,
that I was given the power to say what you felt.
But I see it differently
now that you've gone ahead of me into death,
now that it's me left speechless:
we were taking turns.

The Eldest

After my brother died, I stared out the window.
Then I opened the front door
and looked into the street. There was no use
eating, eating was for fools.
I took a vacation: I went to an island
to think about dying. I drank a bottle of wine.
Then I admitted I knew it would happen:
he had been wild and hurt and so lost
no one could have saved him.
But not until it did
was it obvious
my mother would also die.
And so would my father. Which is why I wept:
I would be the last one.

Landscape with Osprey and Salmon

Rain ticks upon the ferns, over which,
if you listen carefully, the osprey's cries
alert the others that it's found the salmon,
now colored ash with rot and dragged to rocks

where the bird pulls at the elastic flesh.
Another salmon skeleton draped upon a log
hangs like a feather boa left out in the rain
and the skin that once contained it has slid off

like something silk. Rapture joins the world
and irony divides, and unaware of either
the osprey desperately undresses every bone
and then unbuttons both the eyes.

He Who Made the Lamb Made Thee

Later we were taught about original sin
but as children, I remember when we found it.
That's what we did as children: we looked for things
after dinner was over, as the sun was going down,
when the sidewalk was like a pan just taken off the burner.
You found it first, and I made you show me where
in the field: the cat's limp body, the flies.
You who loved animals more than humans
choked as you told me you'd seen the older boys
take turns with the board. We lived in a world
without history, we lived in a suburban development.
Nature crept up to its edges. The cat
didn't have to be lost and soon you
would break down doors, bang your fist into windows
and mirrors and even my face
as you turned into something no one could tame.
Earlier that day we had plucked honeysuckle
and sipped the tiny mouths.

The Ascension

Two feet with delicate toes point down
to the astonished heads of twelve apostles.
Clouds interrupt the blue robe,
and the painting's frame interrupts
everything above the clouds.
                                    Still, you know
it's Christ caught rising in midair,
and that you've been asked to ponder thresholds,

when what happens next is inevitable but also

withdraws a little.
                            But not this
stopped second, no —
and so you must keep looking.
And when you look away, you'll still be a witness
to disappearing instants, you too will be
an apostle of the now.

Landscape with Parking Lot

In some corner of this desert plateau,
native habitat to the partly run-over soda bottle,
freckled with spilled antifreeze
and pied patches of putrid something or other,

a plastic bag is snagged like a tumbleweed
in a perfect cube of hedge.
At night, heat radiates off concrete like an exhale of relief
in this legendary place of the soul's temptation —

Here is where a man agonizes over whether to enter the convenience store
for a six-pack. And where the first can of beer is consumed, then tossed
into the huge anonymous trash can.
Here is where a woman applies lipstick in the rearview mirror
with tears streaming down her face.
Here countless burritos are wolfed down
from greasy paper bouquets held up to the drivers' faces.

They are vast spaces
organized with painted lines, they are not made for you to linger, they
have ingress and egress patterns to move you
efficiently out. And yet the eyes of cell phone users
show with little blinks
the concentration with which they listen elsewhere.
And music lovers linger with the engine running,
waiting for the song to end.

You would think there is only so long you could stay here,
stretching the threshold, delaying what inevitability awaits
inside or beyond, but moments accrue the way the grackles
gather at sunset, landing endlessly one by one on the electric line,
never running out of room to fit another, yet another.

Rescue

Never again will you run that fast
from the black sedan with no headlights
creeping behind you on the walk home.
You were just a girl, but always
you will recall its attentiveness,
how the accelerator gunned
when your lungs ballooned
and you took off running, never again will you
run so beautifully, flying through the dark,
your long hair lashing your cheeks
as you turned back to look.

Never again will you return
to that field by a lone Lutheran church
where an unwalked maze of sidewalks
built for a neighborhood that didn't yet exist
led to the streets where the two of you grew up,
where your shoes' slapping on pavement was the only sound
above the sprinklers' swiveling ticks, where you
cut through empty lots that gaped like missing teeth
in the rows of pale brick houses.

All of your life you will measure every fear
to this first one that sent you sprinting,
you will measure every joy
to the thrilling surge
fear sent down your chest and into your legs.
And how that surge came back up,
your face burning when the car caught up with you,
pulling crookedly into your family's driveway.

Never again will the night feel so mysterious, never
again will your predator be so innocent,
just a little boy, your blond brother,
slumped in the driver's seat
in tears because you ran from him.
Never again will you run from him.
Never again will he come to find you.

Landscape with Arson

Have you ever watched a cigarette released from a driver's fingers
swim through the night air and disintegrate in tiny embers?
Invisible by day, fire's little shards, its quiet dissemination.

That's how, one hot afternoon, no one noticed when
something desperate made the boy devise the strategy
to siphon gas from the motorcycle with a discarded straw,

spitting mouthfuls into a fast-food cup until there was enough
to set the apartment complex on fire.
It happened in a neighborhood at the edge of town

where the wind sifted a constant precipitation of dust
like desiccated snow and the newly poured streets
looked like frosting spread across the desert field.

Ducks had just found the man-made pond.
At dusk, they waddled ashore
to explore the construction site, like the boy.

He started with the door. Stood mesmerized
as the flame took on new colors. He fed it litter
collected from the field. It hissed and turned green,

it splintered pink, it bloomed aureoles of blue.
But there was hardly time to admire it before
remorse overtook him and he fled.

Before the howl of sirens. He was
gone before—he started with the door—whatever
he wanted to let out.

Something can stop being true in the time it takes
a cigarette to burn to its filter. It was your crime
but it's me who goes back to the scene. Now it's only me

who wants to burn something for you, but there's nothing left—how
do you set fire to the past? Only an impulse to shake free—like cellophane
peeled from a pack—something that clings.

Sometimes I conjure a fire for you in my mind,
the gnats swarming furiously above the water, up and down,
can you see it? How they mimic flame, hovering

at the pond's edge. Lately I find myself there all the time.

The Woodstove

The woodstove is banked to last the night,
its slim legs, like an elegant dog's, stand obediently
on the tile floor while in its belly a muffled tumult
cries like wind keening through the hemlocks.

Human nature to sleep by fire, and human nature
to be sleepless by it too. I get up to watch
the blue flames finger soft chambers in the wood
while the coals swell with scintillating breaths.

What made Rousseau once observe that dogs will not
build fires? (And further, that in the pleasing warmth
of a fire already started, they will not add wood?)
What is it to be human? To forge connection,

to make interpretations of fire and contain them
in a little iron stove? And what is it to be fire?
To burn with indifference, to consume
the skin of the arm as easily as the bark of a log.

Sleepy warmth begins to fill the room in which
life wants to live and fire wants to burn,
the room which in the morning
will hold a fire changed to cooling ash.

Outside, smoke escapes and for an instant
mirrors nature too, the way falling snow
reveals the wind's mind, and change of mind,
before world and mind grow inscrutable again.

The Field

There was a dirt field I'd walk to as a girl,
past the convenience store and the train tracks
where the day laborers congregated with six-packs,
where the two-lane road turned to one lane with yellow stripes
and the vacant field loomed like a desiccated fallen sky.

That's where I'd go to sit on an oblong rock
until prairie dogs sprouted from tunnels underground
and the ground became a fabric
stitched by fluid lines of ants.
And though barely perceptible,

if I waited long enough,
the world would begin its shallow breathing,
the soundless wind's only duty in that field
to rearrange a few grains of sand
while the smell of hot dust grew sharp in the nose.

I waited. I don't know for what.
Sometimes I'd sit so long the sun would sink,
a fiery stare blinking shut beneath the horizon,
and the drooping electric wires would borrow the dark
until the dark seeped back into the sky. And when stars

surfaced like needles piercing through velvet,
I'd hold myself back just a moment more.
What made me feel watched in the naked field?
I was paying close attention and could discern only
a begging to be cloaked and a begging to be released.

The Fly

In the café, the fly moves so slowly
I seem to help it along a little when my palm
grazes it in flight. Jesus spoke of the sparrows,
how God loved every one of them,

but in West Texas, the Lutheran pastor of my childhood
preached about the flies, the frenzied gangs
that orbit potato salad turning toxic in the sun
and cause a horse to twitch its eye.

Once he delivered a sermon about a fly
that landed on his windshield at a stop sign, how determined
he was to get rid of it, flooring the accelerator,
his speed increasing with his admiration

for this tiny creature that at 50 mph
still clung to the glass. Let your faith be like a fly
on the windshield of God, he instructed.
And we pondered this from the wooden pews.

But here, far from Texas, the afternoon has slowed down enough
for the café to glow like a sun-streaked jar of honey
and there's a quiet instant between each breath
that isn't inhale or exhale, but where what's neglected

interposes itself, like this portly buzzer
who surveys the sprinkle of sugar crystals and cake crumbs
one table at a time, who makes a faith
from not knowing where to land.

III

The Mountain

I walked up the mountain until I was not an I
is how I might explain it. The wildflowers leaned
backward when a pickup growled by at great speed
and I walked on the gravel edge of the blacktop,
in and out of shade. I don't know how it was so
but I can assure you that for once
there was no Jennifer at all next to the creaking pines,
and when a lumber truck, empty of cargo, thundered up the road,
I rippled with the flowers and then stood frozen
like the vixen farther up the road, one paw lifted in attention.
It was not this way with you, that other mountain
I seemed to climb outside of time, never understanding
its true form or height. I climbed you and you climbed me
is how I might describe it. My feet felt the ground,
and felt it again, and the more I walked
the more that mountain shaped me. Halfway up
I considered this while sitting on a rock,
for the mountain was steep and it had become sad to think
that to be a Jennifer meant to chase endlessly after desire
or else to try to live without it.

When I started up again, I started more slowly,
immersed now in what you might call searching the soul,
not that the soul is a bright red ball
that bounces into the tall grass of a sloping field
but rather the field itself, with all the busy quiet
of the field, the insects humming and even the cigarette butts,
so poorly understood, weathering slowly
into fuzz underground. I could say this much about myself:

much that is dubious and dark still clings to me,
but what I once loved, I love no longer.
Or rather, I still perhaps love, but at least
with discreet moderation. But actually
this is not so, because I love stubbornly
and filled with shame. I am trying to tell the truth.
I love what I long not to love and what I would in fact
like to hate. And I have done this for years,
housed two adversaries who have
strengthened themselves purely in fighting
each other, like two gleaming boxers articulating
a problem to be solved in twelve timed rounds.

I had by this time nearly forgotten where I was
and saw between the trees the glacial lake
that rested at the top of this mountain,
its flat horizon interrupted only by broken trunks
protruding from the water. On the shore an old campfire
blended a pile of sand and ash into grains so fine
a fingertip might compress them to silk.
And among a few caved-in paper cups, a glittering
tangle of magnetic tape unwound from a cassette,
its shiny tendrils scraping across the sand.
I spent several minutes there, seeing the world
and forgetting the self and then seeing the self
and forgetting the world, the world that was
a mountain lake with the remnants
of a beachfront barbecue, and the self saturated with a joy
like melted butter absorbed into a paper plate.
And though I memorized all of this to tell you,
as I am doing now, I felt regardless of what
I might succeed to describe,
I had come upon it all too late.

Ghost

If a boat on water
asked the water to be still:
that's the nature of my want.
You wash over me in gusts.

Few things can be held in hand,
fewer than in the mind.
And the heart, holder
of innumerable devotions,

has no compass, only scale
to overcome the soul's
indifference. The eyes are doors
but otherwise are useless.

There are many ways
to navigate, to be misled.
So I will be restless.
No, I will be still.

Aubade

A bee flew up my dress
and stung my thigh
at the exact moment I was thinking of you.
That was your first try.

The second attempt came at night on a plane.
The head of a stranger dozing in the next seat
drifted to rest on my shoulder. While
ethereal moss spread across the oval window,

you willed your way inside me
through each electric nudge.
When I opened my eyes, the crystals of ice
had pooled into pressurized streams

coursing in veins off the glass.
We descended into morning.
But you lingered during the long glide
back to earth and its weather.

Then the plane's shadow
reached the ground, zooming into worldsize,
covering everything below it without distinction,
darkening green fields and parking lots.

The shadow spilled under the plane
just before we touched down.
You were gone by the time
the wheels kissed the ground.

The Ocracoke Ponies

No one saw the first ones
swim ashore centuries ago,
nudged by waves into the marsh grasses.

When you look into their faces, there is no trace
of the ship seized with terror, the crashing waves
and the horses' cries when thrown overboard.

Every afternoon you ride your bicycle to the pasture
to watch the twitch of their manes and ivory tails
unroll a carpet of silence, to see ponies lost in dream.

But it isn't dream, that place
your mind drifts to, that museum of memory
inventoried in opposition to the present.

You felt it once on a plane,
taking off from a city you didn't want to leave,
the stranded moment when the plane lifts into the clouds.

That's not dream, it's not even sleeping.
It is the nature of sleeping to be unaware.
This was some kind of waiting for the world to come back.

The Clouds

If in arctic ocean huge icebergs crumbled
and piercing light shot up through water,
that's how earth could approximate sky.
I'm lying on the ground again, looking up,
trying to discern layers of clouds overlapping,
trying to see from the ground what I have seen
from a plane passing through their mist, how
some are tall and deep as caverns. They are
nothing like the innumerable pebbles trawled by ants,
the utterly specific grains of sand and
blades of grass impossible to fathom
in their own right. And yet
whatever it is to be on earth includes the clouds
marbling the unadulterated blue.
A soundless explosion of white
that sometimes parts to leak the sun,
occluding stars, blackening with storm,
when do they complete their solemn procession?
I have done this since I was a child,
wonder where they are going, as if
they were the ones that wouldn't last.

The Jetty

It is incorrect to say, "The dark clouds above
bloom full-blown roses." Unless
superbly engorged roses are terrifying to you,
and fascinating, but also ordinary,
in fact, hardly seen. And here, on this jetty
that points toward the blue abyss
where freight ships disappear,

it is imprecise to say the gulf water sings,
that it is a very old song
roughly sung this rainy afternoon. Because here
there is no music, just a soft monotonous roar
the waves spill across the rocks, a liquefaction of lace,
I think, though I know the water's cold and mindless,
that the waves touch blindly, that they continue
like desire, forcing forward until spent.

But if you follow the stray cat
that picks his way upon the rocks
to the beach where the sandpipers run forward to the edge of wet
left when the waves withdraw
                        then hop backward
when the waves rush in, it will be precise to say
that an afternoon is when what it was you had wanted turns
unfamiliar. And when the rain

percusses across the jetty, mixing with the waves
until it seems to be falling upward,
it will be correct to state
that the tall beach grasses lean down
because all day the wind subdues them.

Love Poem with Candle and Fire

Below the flame, the candle warps softly. With you
I am finally alone. Two sadnesses one night in winter

watching the Shanghai burn across the street.
Through the frosted window of our upstairs studio,

the fire flicked orange reflections in ice.
The engines, the sirens, lights circling the bare walls,

the perceptible drifting of smoke.
These are words written by a candle burning.

Here is my breath flickering the flame,
the mind and the body never wanting to be one.

Your arms around me as we faced the window,
I said the flame was impossible to understand

as the shapes of letters before learning to read.
I said, *I love you like the number five in gold* . . .

Why is the mind so restless? Why does the body twitch?
Had there been no separation, if mind and body

silently married, how would I want you as
I do? Now I will be a little fire.

The Record

Kisses too tasted of iron
the year we lived in twilights. They tilted warily
like bags of groceries I'd carry up the stairs
to find you in boxers, the smell of coffee mixed with vinegar
from the bowl of pickle juice you soaked your fingers in
trying to hurry the calluses. We trafficked in the grief
of incompatible day and night, we stretched the hours
as best we could, but mostly we practiced
a kind of starving, excruciating to recall
how hard we tried. I'd unpack the groceries
and tell you about the day, and after dinner
you'd pick out a tune on the guitar
(it was the year you apprenticed to the blues).
Before each night shift, in uniform and socks,
you'd climb into bed and hold me until I fell asleep.
Then you would slip quietly out.
And when I dreamed, I glimpsed the gods in you,
I dreamt you were Hephaestus with the iron forge,
the sweat covering you when you jogged home
was holy, it was the sweat of the whole city,
even the roses, even the bus exhaust.
The mind circles back like a record spinning,
a little molten, a little wobbly, a record
shiny as your black hair, a record player
crackling and stuttering over a scratch, an urge
to ask forgiveness even though it's dark now
and you've already forgiven me.

Mistral

Provençal for *master*, it snakes across the water,
it cleans the haze that stalled the dawn
and folds each page of wave.

On land it acts like water, a deluge or a river,
rushing sediment and paper down
streets and alleyways.

It's Provençal for *master*, that's why
it knocks you over just a little, then holds you close
as water does

when standing in the ocean. It lifts
tablecloths and napkins, ravishes leaves
and unlatched shutters,

spreads dandelion clocks
and the prayers of Tibetan flags. Only plane trees
defy it

with their bony-elbowed branches,
they reach up to feed the sky's blue flame
that weakens anyway to orange.

After the sun comes down and stains the stones, after
it electrifies the grass,
the mistral dons a cloak of stinging velvet

and focuses the stars. And when it goes
nothing comes

                        and jolts you through the air,
nothing flings you like a hook through the snagless air.

Pharos

You traveled so far to see what wasn't there — to see
where it wasn't.

And when you arrived, there was nowhere
to rest your eyes. Everything was moving, even the ground,

in a tide of soapy waves that brooms herded out of shops
and onto the street in late afternoon.

A whole city block jostled violently
under the arm of a man carrying a long mirror.

The lighthouse shone a thousand years ago. Oil-fed flames
surrounded by sheets of bronze

reflected light the way sound rumbles from a cymbal.
Now there is only a ricochet

of sound, five times a day, the muezzin's call, and the men arriving
to spread a carpet right in the street to pray,

one man always standing behind to peel back the carpet
flung up by the wind and flagellating the devoted in the back row.

And the dust, busy as bacteria, embedded even
into the fur of alley cats in its compulsion to cover all.

Everything was moving except the animals
hanging in the butcher shop,

where skinned flesh surrounded the frozen tyranny of eyes
asking, What did you come for?

And the crimson-stained bones answering, That it ever
existed at all is what must sustain you.

Medusa

The first impression is of the curdling of a face.
The second is an awe at the gall he had to paint it,
Caravaggio, and on a shield, a kind of curse
on the viewer frozen into staring, first
at the crumpled brow, then the perfect whites of the eyes
punctured by brown irises looking down,
and then the lips, glistening. And then of course
there are the snakes, so many of them,
squirming in cascades as if trying to get free of
the very head they sprout from.
                         Radiating terror,
I think. That's what you were like, a single strand
snapped free, a little shock
unburied in red clay in the last moment before winter.

I didn't know what I was looking at, what my stare awoke,
metallic blue coil that snapped like a rubber band
and disappeared downward in the ground.
You sprung the way anger lashes out
before it knows its own source and now you are
the quiet afterward that translates what it means to say.
But you were frightened, like the face of the Medusa,
frightening and afraid at once, though I did not see this
in your face but in the skin's elastic glimmer,
a silver-colored belly I caught the barest glimpse of.

I didn't know what I was looking at, and still don't, and I
did not look you in the face, but in my mind
I keep addressing you, thing-that-requires-itself-to-remain-hidden.

The tension between humanity and nature is that
humanity assigns meaning to nature
while nature assigns the most intricate indifference.
To combine them produces a Medusa, I think. And then I think it again,
God, that I do not believe in you. And when I ask myself whom I say that to,
I imagine nothing I have ever encountered
but some slippery thing that flashes in the instant it is gone.

Most Persons Do Not See the Sun

It beats, we say, so relentlessly at the end of June.
And the peonies on the path wait like people at a parade,
like people straining to see what's just out of view,
which this morning is the river, no louder than a whisper,
summer's heat taking a little more of it each day.

Rough stones now snag the flowing silk of the rapids
where water had voluptuously poured in spring, and smooth
rocks lodged in the riverbed emerge like teeth.
Whatever was desperate in its turbulence patiently insists,
now that the river's at its most meager, toward what?

When you take the path lined with peonies that leads to the river
and wade in, you step upon a bed of ancient coins,
flecked with gold and silver mica brighter under the water's lens.
When you stroke absent-mindedly toward the one place
still too deep to touch bottom, you interrupt the confetti of blossoms

the current carries on its surface, the leaves it carries below.
And when it glitters like this it's impossible
to take one's eyes off the water, one is always
glimpsing something just escaping, to love water is to love
light, the sun that beats down and ignites the leaves from within.

You look everywhere except up—the place the eye
was trained to avoid. Turner, who was unafraid,
who said it was like staring at a candle, exclaimed before dying,
"The Sun is God!" But what is the name for
when the water's opaque blue lifts with a ripple

to expose transparent green beneath, or how
the peonies on the path are individually visited by
the ants that eat away the glue that binds them —
so that they are let down like a spill of hair,
petals aired for just a day or two — they hardly last.

Sunrise in Cassis

At its most dull before dawn, the sea's
a stubble field of light still covered with the moony film
pink dawn sponges away.

This is the hour when the moon is a fishhook
steadily pulled up out of the liquid sky
into some drier realm.

And the doves dart and crisscross as if bustling
to take their places on stage,
which does nothing to change that this is the hour

one laughs least. The hour of cold floors,
of pupils adjusting in the early light.
The hour waiting begins for something

one recognizes only after it's passed.
So while the blue of the sea blends with the horizon
I ask to understand the difference between silence and

indifference. I ask time to be wise as an editor,
not to elide this hour
when bakeries pile loaves

in the glass cases and cafés
reassemble their tables and chairs,
hour that converts night's regret

back into gratitude, beautiful hour
when the last few fishing boats sneak out of harbor
to retrieve the nets that wait at the bottom of the sea.

Acknowledgments

Thank you to the editors of the following journals, where some of these poems first appeared, sometimes in slightly different versions:

AGNI: "Late Summer"

American Poetry Review: "The Nunnery"

Cave Wall: "The Clouds," "The Eldest"

Gulf Coast: "Mistral"

Cincinnati Review: "The Ascension," "The Window at Night"

Image: "The Field," "The Icon"

Laurel Review: "Silence"

Literary Imagination: "Aubade," "He Who Made the Lamb Made Thee"

New England Review: "Alchemy," "The Pearl," "Landscape with Town Square," "The Cigarette," "The Ocracoke Ponies," "Love Poem with Candle and Fire," "The Jetty," "The Woodstove," "Landscape with Arson," "Medusa," "The Fly"

Pleiades: "Ghost"

Ploughshares: "Landscape with Parking Lot"

Smartish Pace: "The Umbrella"

Southern Review: "The Mountain," "The Record"

TriQuarterly: "Sunrise in Cassis," "Boy Playing Violin," "Pharos"

"Not Body" appeared in the anthology *Legitimate Dangers: American Poets of the New Century*, Sarabande Books, 2006.

"The Record" appeared in *Best American Poetry 2009*, guest edited by David Wagoner, Scribner, 2009.

"The Ocracoke Ponies" appeared in the anthology *Horse Poems*, Everyman's Library Pocket Poetry, Alfred A. Knopf, 2009.

"The Field," "The Jetty," and "Landscape with Arson" were reprinted on Poetry Daily (www.poems.com).

"The Ocracoke Ponies" is for Lee Zacharias.

"Medusa" is for Ellen Bryant Voigt and Brooks Haxton.

"Pharos" is for Hosam Aboul-Ela.

"Sunrise in Cassis" is for—and after—Adam Zagajewski.

"Silence," "The Eldest," "He Who Made the Lamb Made Thee," "Rescue," and "Landscape with Arson" are in memory of my brother, Eric Lawrence Grotz, 1974–2006.

The book's epigraph is taken from Zbigniew Herbert's "To Take Objects Out," from *Mr. Cogito*, translated by Bogdana and John Carpenter (Oxford University Press, 1993).

My utmost gratitude to Artur Szlosarek and Adam Zagajewski, who introduced me to the poetry of Krakow and to whom this book is dedicated; to Tony Hoagland, Rich Levy, and James Longenbach, for careful, immeasurably generous, and helpful readings of early versions of these poems and of the manuscript as a whole; to Lillie Robertson, C. Dale Young, and Patrick Phillips, for their loyal friendship and poetic support of various kinds; and to Michael Collier and Ellen Bryant Voigt, for their literary vision and guidance that have made such a tremendous difference in my life.

Many of these poems were written with the support of money and time from Inprint, Inc., the Fellowship of Southern Writers, the Camargo Foundation, and the Rona Jaffe Foundation.